American Summer

SEASIDE-INSPIRED RUGS & QUILTS

By Polly Minick

American Summer

SEASIDE-INSPIRED RUGS & QUILTS

By Polly Minick

American Summer
SEASIDE-INSPIRED RUGS & QUILTS

By Polly Minick

Editor: Deb Rowden
Designer: Brian Grubb
Photography: Maria E. Carey
and Aaron T. Leimkuehler
Illustration: Eric Sears
Technical Editor: Kathe Dougherty
Production assistance: Jo Ann Groves

Published by: Kansas City Star Books
1729 Grand Blvd., Kansas City, Missouri, USA 64108

All rights reserved • Copyright © 2012 Polly
Minick and The Kansas City Star Co.

No part of this book may be reproduced, stored
in a retrieval system, or transmitted in any form
or by any means, electronic, mechanical, photo-
copying, recording or otherwise, without the
prior consent of the publisher. Exception: we
grant permission to photocopy the patterns for
personal use only.

No finished quilts or other projects featured in
this book can be produced or sold commercially
without the permission of the author and publisher.

First edition, first printing
ISBN: 978-1-61169-035-4
Library of Congress Control Number:
2011943257

Printed in the United States of
America by Walsworth Publishing Co.,
Marceline, MO

To order copies, call StarInfo at
(816) 234-4636 and say "Books."

PickleDish.com
The Quilter's Home Page
www.PickleDish.com

Acknowledgements

Thanks to our staff at Kansas City Star Quilts – Deb Rowden, Brian Grubb, Eric Sears, Kathe Dougherty, Aaron Leimkuehler, Jo Ann Groves and of course, Doug Weaver and Diane McLendon.

A special thanks to Davey DeGraff for her continued help. She is always able to take my very small and "not so good" sketches and know exactly what I am trying to say. I always say, I could not do this without you.

Luanne Lea for her willingness to drop any other work to sew my binding on my linens so I can get hooking - Thanks Luanne!

To Moda/United Notions, as Laurie and I love working with you on our fabric and wool collections. A special thanks for your continued support and help with our Injured Marine Semper Fi project (see page 94).

Thanks to my friend Sally Siebold who not only collects my work, but was generous to let us shoot photos at her Nantucket home. Thanks, Sally, you are special.

To our cousin Nancy Neutgens, thanks for taking time to make the beach ball for this book using Minick and Simpson fabric.

Michelle Reed - friend and photographer - for always finding time in her busy schedule to take studio shots of the rugs.

Maria Carey, friend and photographer - who took great care and spent lots of her valuable time to shoot the pieces for us on our shores at Naples and Nantucket.

Cam Dutton, owner of Nantucket Country, who hosts my annual rug sale each summer at her gallery, which has allowed me to meet so many wonderful residents of Nantucket.

Edyth O'Neill, designer of the America rug on page 12, thank you for allowing me to tweak it a bit and add it to my book.

To my family - who is always supportive and my constant cheerleader! They make me think, "I can do anything." You mean the world to me.

To Laurie Simpson, my talented sister, for her wonderful contributions to this book - it is great fun working together on all we do.

And, most important, my husband Tom – for supporting and encouraging me. He is always willing to help in any way - proofreading, steaming rugs – you name it, he will help.

Laurie would like to thank:

Leigh Ann Prange - the perfect "go-to" person when you want a pillow finished or a bag made.

Kari Smith Ruedisale - for her exquisite machine quilting.

Lisa Christensen - for her ingenuity in putting all my ideas into digital form.

Contents

Polly Minick

About the Author

Polly Minick began hooking rugs in the 70's – by hook or crook she was determined to accomplish this feat. Being an avid antique collector, she wanted a couple of rugs to go with her collections. The rugs she saw at antique shows were not always in great condition, so she decided to make her own. She felt no need for lessons or that this would be a serious undertaking - she just wanted to make the rugs and be done with it. What she found along the way was that making those two rugs look like what she envisioned was going to take a little longer than she anticipated. She also found that she was "hooked" on rug hooking.

Polly and her husband Tom live in Naples, Florida, with their Airedale Annie and love life along the coast. They have three sons and seven grandchildren they love to keep company with - the grandkids also love their current location of Naples.

Since she started making rugs Polly has garnered praise in articles in: *Better Homes and Gardens, Country Home, Coastal Living, Architectural Digest, Colonial Homes, Early American Life, Victoria, Creative Home, American Patchwork and Quilting, Romantic Homes,* and *Elle Décor. The New York Times, Houston Chronicle, George Towner, The Islander, Naples Daily News,* and *Ann Arbor News* have also written of her accomplishments.

Polly is a primitive rug hooker and like many other primitive rug hookers, she draws inspiration from what is around her. She is inspired by family, home, country and nature. Her imagery includes stars, flags, hearts and houses. Her patriotic works were inspired when their youngest son Jim received a commission in the United States Marine Corps; he is currently serving our country as a Colonel and recently returned from his second tour in Iraq. Jim's service has also inspired her to work diligently for the Semper Fi Injured Marine Fund which she says is "a labor of love."

The whimsy of Polly's motifs and patterns is understandable given her aim to stick to her goal of making her rugs primitive and naïve. She describes many of her drawings as "childlike," placing strong emphasis on her respect and appreciation for early-American creations.

Polly's enthusiasm for the art has led to national acclaim as a creator of primitive-style rugs and a highly touted guest lecturer. She enjoys traveling the country and meeting with others who also love fiber art. She is proud of the increased interest in this fiber art over the years, and she feels a responsibility for its continued growth.

American Summer celebrates Americans' love affair with vacations by the shore.

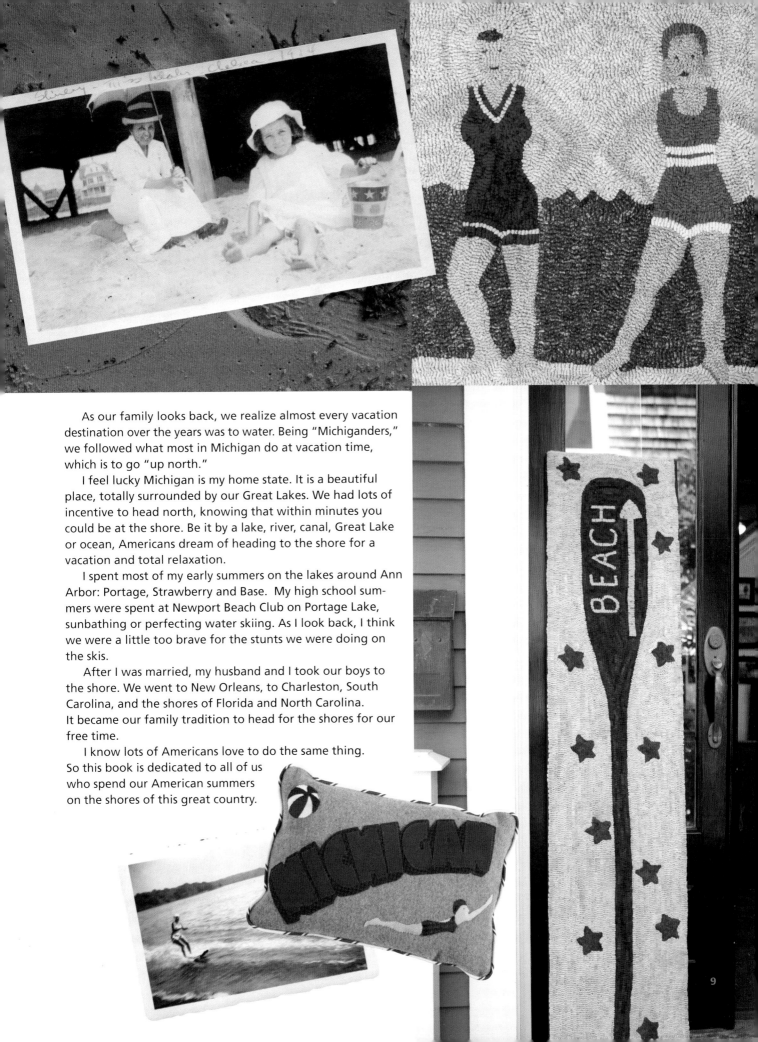

As our family looks back, we realize almost every vacation destination over the years was to water. Being "Michiganders," we followed what most in Michigan do at vacation time, which is to go "up north."

I feel lucky Michigan is my home state. It is a beautiful place, totally surrounded by our Great Lakes. We had lots of incentive to head north, knowing that within minutes you could be at the shore. Be it by a lake, river, canal, Great Lake or ocean, Americans dream of heading to the shore for a vacation and total relaxation.

I spent most of my early summers on the lakes around Ann Arbor: Portage, Strawberry and Base. My high school summers were spent at Newport Beach Club on Portage Lake, sunbathing or perfecting water skiing. As I look back, I think we were a little too brave for the stunts we were doing on the skis.

After I was married, my husband and I took our boys to the shore. We went to New Orleans, to Charleston, South Carolina, and the shores of Florida and North Carolina. It became our family tradition to head for the shores for our free time.

I know lots of Americans love to do the same thing. So this book is dedicated to all of us who spend our American summers on the shores of this great country.

The Basics
Supplies Needed

Hoop or Frame

Use a frame or hoop to keep backing fabric taut as you hook. I find I cannot work fast if fabric is not taut. And yes, you can hook without a frame or hoop - I have a friend who does that. I know it seems strange and difficult, but it can be done. They simply roll their fabric and hold it in such a way that it works for them. It's painful for me to watch, but all choices are pretty personal. Most rug hookers use a frame. I use a hoop and that is all I have ever used and I am sticking with it. If I am at a "hook-in" or a workshop, most everyone there (I would say 99%) uses a frame.

A hoop holds the backing taut by putting the backing over the bottom round of the hoop. The top round is placed over your piece and tightened down with the screw mechanism on the top of hoop. It works fine for me - I feel more portable and comfortable with a hoop.

A frame has grippers on the sides. You lay your rug over the bottom piece with grippers and you then tighten the frame. There are many different types of frames and all are a little different in how you tighten them.

All supplies are very personal choices and each artist will find what is more compatible with one or the other. When I teach, I always take a very beginner hoop and hook and let students try them and others that are in the classroom, as it is best you try a few before you decide. You should know if you are sticking with this art before you spend any more money so it is nice to be able to try many different styles. This goes back to my tip on "test driving" the supplies (page 15). Once an artist has chosen what they feel most comfortable with, you will rarely get them to change.

Hook

I use a primitive hook. It is a hook with a simple short wooden handle with a flat area for my thumb. The hook itself is short, thick and not pointed. Some hooks are longer or called pencil handles; some are small hooks; some are pointed (ouch). There are so many wonderful options - find what works for you and treasure it.

Strip Chart

Blade size=strip width

#3=3/32"

#4=1/8"

#5=5/32"

#6=6/32" - 3/16"

#7=7/32"

#8=8/32" - 1/4"

#9=9/32"

Cutter

To get the wool in strips, cut it with scissors or tear it - most use a strip cutter. Many artists, especially if they started out quilting, will continue to use the rotary cutter with no problem. And cutters are more costly than any other supply so if a rotary is working for them, they should continue. Again, this is a personal choice. Many companies make cutters. I use a Townsend. This brand lets you change blade sizes easily. Most cloth strippers have inter-changeable blades that cut from #2 to a size #10 and beyond. I use #8 on 90% of my work. Most traditional artists use #3 - #6 and most primitive art-ists use #8 and above.

Lighting

Lighting is very important. I always use an Ott-Lite - it shows colors clearly. There are other companies that make such lights - check them out.

Rug Backing

I use linen and would say that is the most common backing choice. Other options are burlap, monks' cloth and rug warp. Again, it is a personal choice.

Binding

There are many ways to bind a rug and also many choices of binding material. Some use wool yarn and whipstitch the edges, most use cloth tape to finish a rug. I use these two options:

- black binding tape for rugs with an antique black background, or
- ticking tape (I use this most)

You can also use wool fabric to bind a rug. You can actually use the wool strips, I have done that a couple of times. Use a large needle that can handle your wool strips and stitch away.

The part of binding that is a *must* for me is to sew the binding onto the backing before I pull the first loop. I think this gives a great edge and a nice look. You can hook right up next to the binding that is already attached. When you are done hooking, trim off the excess backing, turn the edge over, and hand stitch it in place.

Transferring Your Design with Red Dot

You will notice the term "red dot" when reading about rug hooking. When a pattern is to be enlarged, take it to a copy center. Ask a staff member to help you enlarge it the amount stated on the pattern. They will set the machine for you and help you copy. You leave the store with a pattern the actual size of the rug and you are ready to transfer. Put the piece of red dot transparent fabric over the enlarged pattern and trace over it with a black magic marker. Then carefully line the red dot fabric on top of your backing choice, and pin the red dot fabric to the backing to hold it in place. Trace over the pattern again with magic marker to put the design on your fabric backing. When you lift the red dot, you will see the pattern on the backing, but it will be faint. Once again, trace over the pattern with magic marker. Now your pattern is on the backing of your choice and you are ready to hook.

Scissors

A great pair of scissors will be a good investment for you in years to come. Many sizes, styles and prices of scissors are available. Find ones that fit your hand and treat them well.

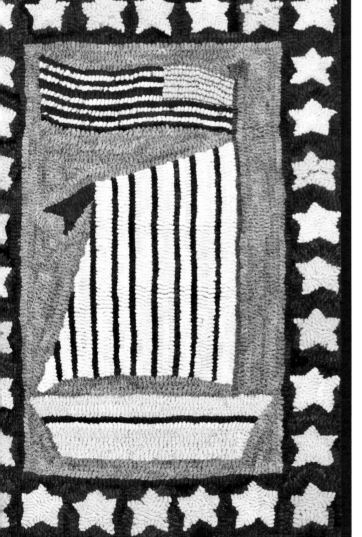

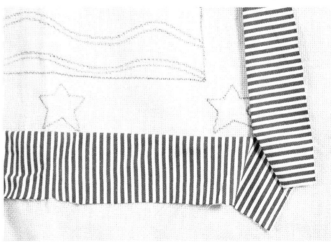

Black Permanent Markers

After reading the paragraph above, you totally understand the need and use of a good set of permanent markers.

Hooking the Rug

Place the piece onto your frame or hoop, making sure it is taut. You are now ready to pull your first loop. Hold the wool strip under the backing with your left hand and with your right hand, pull the loop through the backing to make your first loop. Pull the end of the strip up through the backing and you are on your way. Pull the next loop right up next to the tail you just pulled through. Trim the tail down to the height of your loops (it is best to hook for a bit and trim ends later). For beginners, there is much angst over pulling loops - it seems foreign and makes you nervous. I always say it is like riding a bike or typing – it is hard at first and becomes automatic after a bit of time. Remember to think "do not twist" and pull your loops up to a good height - such as 1/4". It is awkward at first, but it comes along. In the beginning, no one pulls their loops the desired height, but it comes soon.

You are on your way! Remember, you are trying to cover the backing. Do not pack your loops too close - they should be just touching. It sounds like a lot to notice at once, but it is soon automatic and something you will not have to think so much about. You may look back and laugh at the angst it first caused you.

For primitive hooking - we often outline and fill. Sometimes you outline in a different shade than the inner object and sometimes the color is the same, but outline and fill is a concept in primitive hooking. Remember to stay inside the lines. I usually hook the interior images, then the border, and finally the background.

Finishing the Rug

Remember, I sew (or have sewn) the ticking fabric or binding tape first, as this is what works best for me. I feel I can hook close to the binding fabric and get a good straight edge. If this is your choice, when hooking is completed, you simply trim off any excess backing, turn over the fabric or tape and hand stitch it in place for your finished edge. Many whipstitch their edges as we discussed above under Binding. As a non-sewer, this works best for me.

When the binding is on, your first rug is done. You may want to test a few different ways to finish the rug. When you find what is best for you, stick with it.

Signing Your Rug

I use an embroidered tag to sign my rugs. Many artists hook their initials boldly on the front of the rug so it's easy to see. Others work to hide them and you have to search for them, but they are there. There are many options, and again it is a personal choice. I do recommend that you sign your rug in some manner.

Blocking the Rug

Blocking gives a rug a finished look. To do this, lay your rug on a flat surface, cover it with a damp towel and steam with a hot iron. I now have the new "boiler" iron and I like it very much. The new boiler iron lets me steam many rugs in a day if I am getting ready for a show. I find that I have to re-fill the boiler after two rugs, but it works wonderfully. I have a friend who pins her rug into her wall-to-wall carpeting with "t" pins and steams away. Choose the method that works best for you.

Try Before You Buy

Supplies are plentiful so for that very reason my motto is "test drive before you buy." I always tell students that hooks alone come in all sizes and shapes and most artists will eventually find the one that is just RIGHT for them. So before you put your cash on the line, I suggest you ask to test several first - those who sell hooks are most always willing to let you try a hook before you buy. Also for frames - as they seem to offer new designs each year and all have very dedicated owners - try one before you buy. I have never used a frame so I cannot be of help - I started on a hoop and have never wanted to change. Make sure what you choose is the one for you.

Timid to Jump into the Dye Pot??

I know I certainly was timid to get into dyeing. I realized it would take time, effort, money and could make a lasting mess. I fought it for a long time – it was just too scary. As I started hooking more rugs – the desire to get the correct color made me agree to jump in - and it helped I was doing it with friends.

But if you are timid about dyeing, try this. I call it a poor man's dyeing method and I used it for a long time before I took on the task of learning to dye my wool and making my own dye formulas. Marrying colors is a simple way to blend different wool colors so that they are more coordinated - without using any dye. Take several pieces of the same shade, let's say a medium blue. They can be different shades, not totally blending, some clashing. Put a big pot of water on the stove and bring the water to a boil. Add 1 tablespoon detergent (I use Arm and Hammer but am told any will work), then add the wools. After the wool has gently boiled for some time, turn off the heat. Leave the pot on the stove overnight to cool. When the water is boiling the color turns a dark blue - in the morning when cool, the water is perfectly clear.

The boiling process brings color out of all the pieces and as it cools, the color in the water seeps back into the wool. The pieces still are not the same color - all different shades of blue - but they are more "married" or blended and none of the blues clash. The pieces will be different enough to give you nice texture when used together in a rug, but they'll at least look like they came from the same color family.

Tips

Memory Wool

I would like to share a few stories about memory wool. A friend told me that her grandmother, who was an avid rug hooker, talked her out of her favorite tattered baby blanket to hook into a rug for her. Of course the real reason was to get the tattered blanket from her before she started school - but she loves her rug now and loves the story. I used wool from a late friend's favorite outfit into a rug that I treasure. Dealing with the grief of losing a friend, you'll find some comfort in using a favorite piece of their wool in a lasting rug.

A Different View

A digital camera is a good tool for getting an overall look at your piece as it progresses. It helps you identify a color that is "jumping out" and not blending as you would like. If I am in doubt about a color, a photo will reveal that and tell you a change in color is needed.

A friend of mine hangs her piece on a skirt hanger in the doorway. When she walks back in the room the next morning with fresh eyes she can see if the colors are working well or not.

Another idea - if you are having doubts about a color in your piece, I suggest you put it away for a bit and work on something else. When you get the rug out to work on it again, if it is still bothering you, it's time to make a change.

Rug Repair Kit

My late friend, Patty Yoder, shared this tip with me and I am so grateful. She saved some of each of her color strips and some small uncut wool pieces from each rug she made and placed them in a plastic baggie labeled with the name of the rug and the date. If a small repair is needed later, the wool is available and easily identifiable.

Color Variations

Colors that are mentioned in my supply list may say just red. Please keep in mind that when I use any color, for me that color will mean many different wools of that color, some just a little lighter or darker, never clashing. A mixture of similar colors gives the rug movement, texture and looks personally made - not machine made. I always pull the reds I am going to use, cut some from each of the pieces, mix and put in a basket to pull randomly (you will love this tip).

Don't Cut All the Wool at One Time

Please keep in mind that you do not need to cut all the wool in strips when you begin. Keeping track of the cut wool (worms) is not easy, they are determined to tangle for you. Also, it's hard to keep track of wool amounts and what you need to finish when all are cut into strips.

How Much Wool Do You Need?

Each project in this book includes a detailed supply list telling you just how much of each color you will need for your project. If you want to make a design change on a pattern or kit, here's how to figure how much wool you need to hook a particular image. Take the wool you have chosen for that image in the rug, fold it over four times, and lay it on the image you want to hook. If the piece of wool covers the image and is four layers deep, you will have enough wool.

Note that yardage requirements for the projects in this book are all based on this formula. Depending on how closely together you pack the loops, you may need 5 times the amount - you will soon be able to decide the amounts based on your hooking style.

Develop Your Own Style

I feel strongly that a person develops a signature in their rugs after a fashion. Whether you like to hook certain images, have a flair for borders, or always use the same color palette, you are developing your own style. Color is certainly a signature for many artists. Work in the colors you love, not just the colors I have presented. Work in what is really "you."

My advice is to not plan a rug around a wall color or a sofa, as those things change. Your color palette is usually always with you. If you plan a rug with an image you are fond of and colors you love, you will always love the rug.

Do not be frightened by color. Do not let others tell you a certain color is a "must" in a rug - always remember it is your rug and you have to love it. Always listen to suggestions as they are given with best intentions, but do not change your own feelings just to be nice. It is your rug and your personal color choice should be what goes into it.

Borders

Borders can be fun, and they can be a very important part of any rug. A rug without a border is just fine - you will see an equal amount of rugs without borders. I make more rugs with borders than without, but I do like some rugs without a border. If you are going with a border, be creative and have fun with your border. Read on for some tips on borders.

Tips on Borders:

1. I always feel that you should not put color in a border that is not in the main part of rug - it may look like it doesn't fit.
2. Feel free to pull an image from the center of the rug, scale it down and put it in the border.
3. Random stripes in a border is one look that I love and is fun to hook - it was a favorite choice many years back. Striped borders are a happy mix of color and texture and the more the merrier in this case, scrappy is good.
4. Sometimes I use the same background color on a rug as the background color of the border. When you do this, hook a stripe in contrasting color to distinguish the border.
5. Hooking stripes on the diagonal is also nice - but be careful - it can get a little out of whack if you are not careful. Pay attention when hooking.
6. For corners on a border, feel free to block off the corners and then fill in solid color or add a star - it gives a nice touch.

Enlarging Designs

If the design is not the actual size you want your rug to be, you can have the design enlarged at a local copy shop. Fortunately, I've found that most copy shops have staff willing to help with calculators in hand. For instance, if you tell them that you want the length to be no larger than a stated measurement, their calculator can figure this for you. I have tried to do this on my own and a mistake can be costly on the large copiers, so it's best to ask. Also, if you are going to enlarge one of the patterns in this book that states, "enlarge 400%" it is best to copy the page at home, and just take the copy with you as some employees are still unwilling to let you copy a page from a book (even when it is obvious that it was meant for you to copy).

Tips for Success

- Try to keep loops uniform, and at least 1/4" high.

- Do not twist your wool strips. Use your hand below the backing to keep the wool flat on the underside of your rug.

- Do not hook too tightly or your images can become distorted. Skipping one or more holes in the weave of your backing fabric while hooking will keep the loops loose, yet fill in the surface nicely.

- Pull your first tail up thru the top of your backing when starting a new strip - pull your first strip end up and start your next strip in the same hole. Go back and snip the ends later.

- Stay in the lines - as you were told in school, stay within the lines. It works the same for rug hooking - not on the line or beyond, but inside. That will help keep your images as they were drawn.

- If using a hoop or frame, make sure your backing is held taut.

- Do not "carry" your wool across the backing - instead cut and restart.

- Do not hook your backgrounds in a straight line. Outline your images and keep doing that and you will be hooking in the free form that is satisfying. I tell students if you have a large background space away from lines, take a magic marker, make a swirl and hook that and start following that form for a nice effect.

- I always hook the very outside line of my border before I fill in the border. And remember I have my binding or ticking sewn on before I pull one loop - so when getting to the background I will hook that outside line next to the binding fabric - that seems to help keep the form. If you have a line between the center of the rug and your border, it is usually done in a contrasting color. I hook that also before I do the background colors in border.

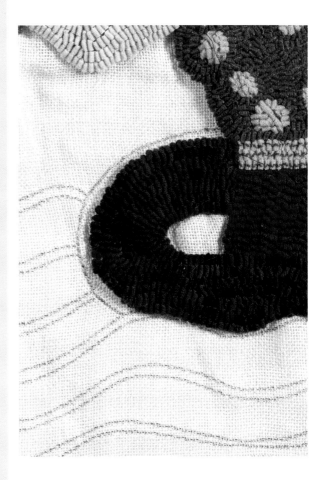

- Usually, start with the center images, then the background and finally the border. However, I have been known to hook the borders first - not often but for some reasons I have done that. Most often you always do the center images first!

- Color Color Color! Often people snicker when I speak of color - as many think of color as bright and varied and I do not. Whatever color you use, please be careful with your choices. Be it dull or muted colors or brighter colors - make sure the colors work together for a pleasing result. I am not known for using bright color. My early rugs were antique black, old red, mustard olive and muted blues - not wild colors. Whatever your color palette is, spend time making sure the colors work well together. Since my move south, I find I use many lighter colors - but I have never used bright colors that so many work wonders with. It just does not work for me.

Read This Before You Start a Rug

Read all these instructions before starting. Look for more specific information with each rug.

Making the Rug

1. Transfer the design onto the backing of your choice. Note that each pattern includes the percentage to be enlarged (such as 400%). Refer to the Basic Rug Hooking Tips on page 10 for more information on the basics. After the design is on your backing, keep the edges from fraying by serging, zigzag stitch, or with masking tape.

2. On each rug, look for recommendations of the order in which to hook the rug elements (example: do the flag and flagpole first, etc).

3. Remember when hooking a fairly large background area (like sky or ocean) to use many shades of the same color. Cut them into strips, mix them up in a basket, then pull them out randomly for a good look. By using more than one shade in a particular color, your rug will show more movement and texture and will look more professional.

Cutting

Cut your wool in #8 strips* (that is my preference – cut strips your favorite size). Don't cut all the wool at one time as strips/worms are prone to tangle and are harder to manage. Also, if all the wool is cut it is more difficult to keep track of materials needed to finish the rug. Wool is much easier to measure in one piece (instead of strips).

*See page 11 of Basic Rug Hooking Tips for a chart of strip sizes.

Materials

Wool yardage estimates are based on 60" wide wool. To estimate the amount of wool needed for an image, fold the wool over 4 times and place it on top of the image to be hooked. That should be enough wool to hook the image.

Finishing the Rug

1. Finish the rug using rug binding tape for fabric. See page 14 for tips on finishing the rug.

2. Steam and block the rug – follow the instructions on page 14 .

3. Be sure to sew an identification tag on your rug. Read my thoughts on signing a rug tag on page 14. There are many ways to sign a rug - it is a personal choice.

Projects

July 4th Parade

24" x 54"

This July 4th rug was lots of fun to plan and hook. I designed this rug with our sons in mind – they were always known as the Minick boys. I remembered all the parades we attended. Now the boys go with their children, so this was fitting for our family. We have always had an Airedale so it was easy to add their current pal in the wagon. Go ahead and personalize this pattern a bit to match your family.

Supply List

Note: all yardage refers to wool unless otherwise noted.

- ❍ 1 3/4 yards mixed navy blue for background and letters
- ❍ 1/2 yard red for border, vest, flags, balloon, wheelbarrow
- ❍ 1/2 yard off-white for vest, sailor suit, balloon, border, tires, wagon, stars
- ❍ 1/8 yard for flesh
- ❍ 1/8 yard gold for flag poles and hair
- ❍ 1/16 yard brown/black for dog
- ❍ 1/16 yard soft blue for bicycle, balloon

- ❍ 1/16 yard off-white wool, or cotton "Dick and Jane" fabric for newspaper hats
- ❍ 1/16 yard light gray for bicycle tires
- ❍ 1/16 yard blue/white check for flag cantons and boy's shirt, boy's pants
- ❍ 1/16 yard red stripe for trim on wagon and wheelbarrow
- ❍ Backing material 40" x 70"* *Measurement reflects 8" added to each side (for use in a hoop)
- ❍ 160" binding tape or 1" – 3" wide fabric to bind

To Make This Rug

- Enlarge this pattern 550%.
- Order: I started with the smaller, more tedious images - the children, balloons, wagon, wheelbarrow, hats and flags. When the center images are completed, I did the background, using a mix of navy blues. Next I did the stars in each corner and then the border. These images are smaller than those I usually hook, but I felt this rug was really worth the work - so enjoy.

ENLARGE 550%

Bathing Beauties

27" x 40"

I have also hooked a version of this rug using only two bathing beauties.

Bathing Beauties came about when my thoughts turned to summer themed rugs - that happened when I started my annual show/sale on beautiful Nantucket. My sister Laurie and I had just designed a summer theme fabric line. We were inspired by photos we found of our mother and her sisters in their swimsuits taken on the lake at their family farm in Michigan. So with American Summer and our beautiful shores in mind, a Bathing Beauties rug was a must!

Supply List

Note: all yardage refers to wool unless otherwise noted.

- ○ 1 1/2 yards soft blue for sky
- ○ 1/2 yard mixture of blues for ocean
- ○ 1/2 yard tan tweed for sand
- ○ 1/4 yard navy blue for border
- ○ 1 3/4 yards red for suits, sand pail and lettering, flag
- ○ 1/16 yard blue for blue bathing suit
- ○ 1/8 yard green for suit
- ○ 8 strips of gold for flag pole
- ○ 1/16 yard blue/white check or tweed for flag canton
- ○ 1/16 yard red for bars on flag
- ○ 1/16 yard off-white bars on flag
- ○ 1/8 yard flesh
- ○ Backing material 38" x 56"*
    *Measurement reflects 8" added to each side (for use in a hoop)
- ○ 128"binding tape or 1" – 3" wide fabric to bind

To Make This Rug

- ○ Enlarge this pattern 300%.
- ○ Order: I started with the flag on this rug. (As you probably are now aware, I love to hook flags and this one was no exception.) I then hooked the gals, and you will notice dimension on their faces – I used the more folk art version, but you can also do just flesh for faces. That is often done and works fine. I then did the sky, ocean and sand last, after I hooked the lettering.

ENLARGE
300%

BATHING BEAUTIES

You cannot spend time on Nantucket and not be aware of Moby Dick and the whaling industry that existed on that island. I decided I needed a whale rug for my show - why not Moby Dick? This fairly simple yet charming rug soon became a big hit at my shows.

Moby Dick 20" x 42"

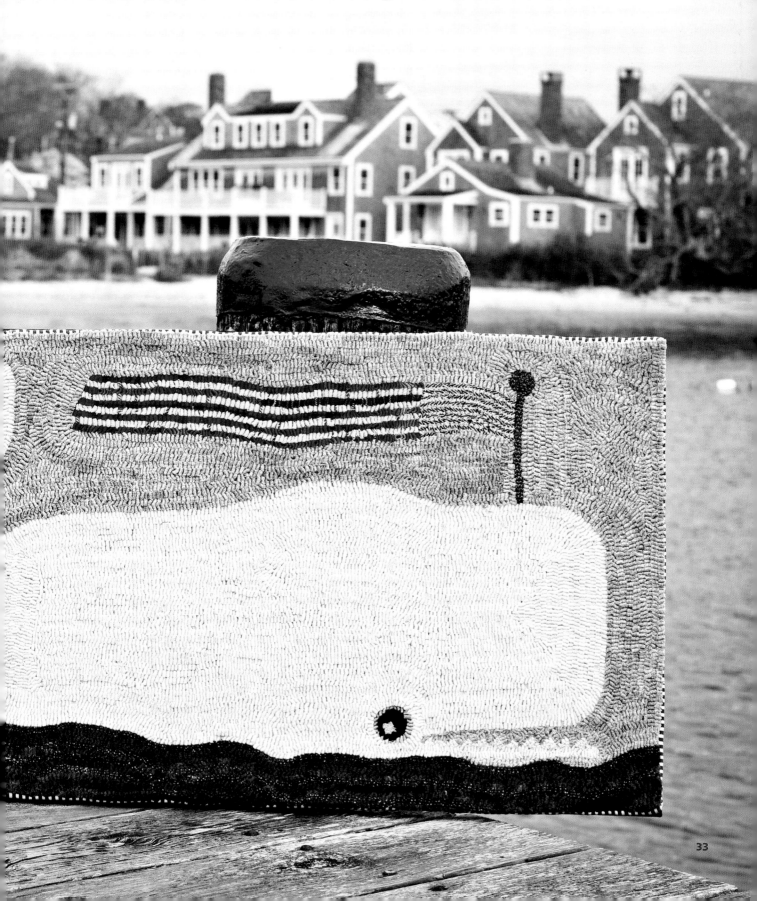

Supply List

Note: all yardage refers to wool unless otherwise noted.

- ○ 1 yard off-white for Moby
- ○ 1 yard soft blue for sky
- ○ 1/4 yard mix of darker blues for ocean
- ○ 8 strips gold for flagpole and star
- ○ 14 strips of whites for flag bars
- ○ 14 strips of reds for flag bars
- ○ 1/16 yard blue/white check for flag canton
- ○ Backing material 36" x 58"*
  *Measurement reflects 8" added to each side (for use in a hoop)
- ○ 128" binding tape or 1" – 3" wide fabric to bind

To Make This Rug

- ○ Enlarge this pattern 400%.
- ○ Order: This is a fun and easy rug to hook, with nice large images. I start with Moby Dick and I have hooked Moby a couple of different ways, but I now prefer the simple, solid off white for Moby – that way you only have to deal with the eye, which most do not like to do. I have found the easiest way to hook the eye is to hook the eye black and add a couple of white loops – which gives you a good look for an eye. The most tedious part of this rug is the teeth: just cut your strips smaller (like a 6 or 7) and make little triangles and you will be fine. Follow up with sky and ocean.

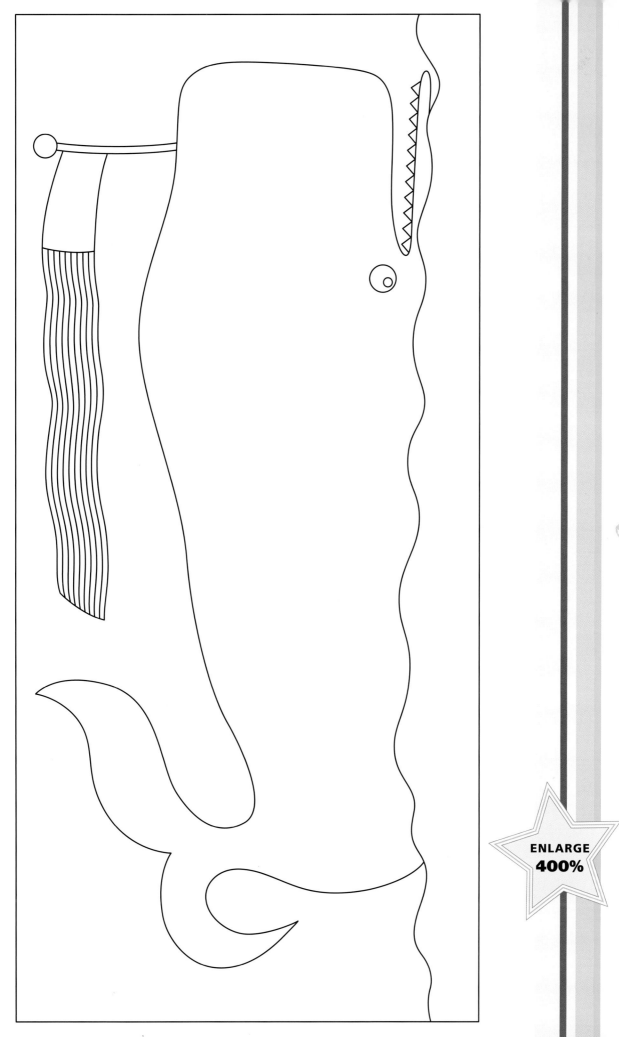

ENLARGE
400%

Seaside 29" x 42"

Seaside or Nantucket is a favorite rug of mine. You can personalize the lettering with a spot that is special to you and your family. I often use the name Seaside as it is generic and it is often used on the early sand pails I love to collect. But after being on Nantucket for the last several summers, I decided I had to have a Nantucket rug!

Supply List

Note: all yardage refers to wool unless otherwise noted.

- ◌ 1 3/4 yard navy blue mix for background
- ◌ 1/2 yard red for flag bars, stars, lettering
- ◌ 3/4 yard off-white for flag bars, swim suit
- ◌ 1/8 yard gold for flag pole, star
- ◌ 1/8 yard blue/white check for lining on suit neckline (arms optional)
- ◌ 1/2 yard soft blue for canton of flag
- ◌ 1/2 yard white with blue stripes for stars (and to use in bars of flag)
- ◌ Backing material needed, 45" x 58"*
  *Measurement reflects 8" added to each side (for use in a hoop)
- ◌ 146" binding tape or 1" – 3" wide fabric to bind

To Make This Rug

- ◌ Enlarge this pattern 400%.
- ◌ Order: Start with the flag and flag pole, then the bathing suit and stars - and you are left with the background. This is a nice rug to own and very easy to hook. What is not to like about large images!!

Tip: I like to leave the background for last. If I am traveling and want to take a piece with me to work on, I only need to pack one color to take along.

NANTUCKET

ENLARGE
400%

Whale Game Board

20" x 35"

This rug favors many things that I love - Nantucket is a special spot in this country for me. And really, a wonderful place to travel to: it is historic, quaint and lovely. As a collector of early game boards and a great admirer of Nantucket - a whale game board was easy to come up with - fun to hook and lovely to hang.

Supply List

Note: all yardage refers to wool unless otherwise noted.

- ❍ 3/4 yard blue for squares on game board
- ❍ 3/4 yard off-whites for squares on game board
- ❍ 1/4 yard grayish-white for whales
- ❍ 1/4 yard soft blue for sky
- ❍ 1/8 yard dark blues mix for ocean, can be dark to bright blue
- ❍ 4 strips black for eyes

- ❍ 6 strips blue/white check for canton on flag
- ❍ 8 strips red for flag
- ❍ 8 strips white for bars on flag
- ❍ 10 strips gold for flagpoles
- ❍ Backing material 36" x 51"*
  *Measurement reflects 8" added to each side (for use in a hoop)
- ❍ 114" binding tape or 1" – 3" wide fabric to bind

To Make This Rug

○ Enlarge this pattern 350%.

○ Order: This is a rug that I hook a little differently than usual. When I teach, I show the best and most accurate way to work. However, I do not always work that way. For instance, in hooking the blocks in the checkerboard, I would teach that you pull up the tail, hook down a row, clip and start the next row at the top, pulling the tails up at the beginning and end of each row. That leaves lots of tails to see from the top of the rug, and these blocks are small. So instead, I start at upper corner of block, bring down - go over one row and go up and carry on - NOT the way I would teach. After finishing the blocks, hook the whales, then the background.

Whale Game Board

20" x35'

ENLARGE
350%

Americans love lighthouses. We are quick to photograph any lighthouse we see while vacationing on our shores. Nantucket is home to three historic lighthouses. They started guiding sailors to their shores in the 1700s - three remain today to offer guidance to those coming ashore. One of the most photographed is Brant Point lighthouse. Our home state of Michigan at one time had over 200 working lighthouses - the number of working lighthouses is now under 100. They will always make us want to pull out our cameras for a photograph.

Brant Point Lighthouse

17" x 34'

Supply List

Note: all yardage refers to wool unless otherwise noted.

- ○ 1/2 yard soft blue for sky
- ○ 1/2 yard darker blue mix for ocean
- ○ 1/4 yard off-white for lighthouse
- ○ 1/8 yard black for lighthouse
- ○ 1/8 yard brown/gray plaids, tweeds for rocks
- ○ 1/8 yard red for ribbon wreath, roof
- ○ 8 strips tan tweed for sand
- ○ 8 strips green mix for wreath
- ○ 8 strips for gray trim on lighthouse
- ○ Backing material 33" x 50"*
  *Measurement reflects 8" added to each side (for use in a hoop)
- ○ 106" binding tape or 1" – 3" wide fabric to bind

To Make This Rug

- ○ Enlarge this pattern 240%.
- ○ Order: I started with the lighthouse, followed by the rocks, ocean and finally the sky. *Note:* we dressed up our lighthouse for the winter holidays - you can hook yours with or without the wreath.

*Round Island Lighthouse,
Mackinac Island, Michigan*

Beach Gal

24" x 32"

I spent my youth in Michigan. We were not without our own beautiful inland lakes and were surrounded by the fabulous Great Lakes! American Summers were spent on lakes, rivers, canals, Great Lakes and oceans - this great land offers up many special places to spend the summer. Beach Gal is a reminder to all of us who vacationed on the water. This gal is on a sea horse, but all of my friends spent time on the water in our tubes. My design inspiration was an antique 1910 noisemaker.

Supply List
Note: all yardage refers to wool unless otherwise noted.

- ❍ 3/4 yard soft blue texture for sky
- ❍ 1/2 yard mixed blues for ocean
- ❍ 1/4 yard red for border
- ❍ 1/4 yard white for border
- ❍ 1/4 yard bright blue texture for stars in border
- ❍ 6 strips gold for flag pole
- ❍ 4 strips gold (or color of your choice) for hair
- ❍ 1/16 yard flesh for girl
- ❍ 1/8 yard red for flag, swimsuit, lips
- ❍ 1/8 yard white for seahorse, flag, cap, eyes, swimsuit belt
- ❍ 1/8 yard blue for seahorse
- ❍ 1/16 yard blue/white for canton, trims
- ❍ 3 strips black for eyes
- ❍ Backing material 40" x 48"*
   *Measurement reflects 8" added to each side
   (for use in a hoop)
- ❍ 116" binding tape or 1" – 3" wide fabric/ticking to bind

To Make This Rug

○ Enlarge this pattern 325%.
○ Order: I started with the gal, flag
   and then seahorse. (You can see
   from photos I also hooked this
   same rug having the gal on an inner
   tube rather than the seahorse -
   both are fun rugs.) I then did the
   ocean, then sky. The border is a
   bit tedious, but worth it.

ENLARGE
325%

Boy on Beach

 27" x 32"

The inspiration for this rug was an old circus poster showing a young boy holding a lollipop. The colors of the old poster were great. One thing I noticed was it had a bunting style border. Having hooked Beach Gal a few months before, I thought we needed a young man on the shore also.

Supply List

Note: all yardage refers to wool unless otherwise noted.

- ❍ 3/4 yard soft blue for sky
- ❍ 1/2 yard red for shovel, bunting, flag, shield, lips
- ❍ 1/2 yard off-white for stars, bunting, suit, flag, pail, shield
- ❍ 1/16 yard tan tweed for sand
- ❍ 3/4 yard navy blue for sailor suit, shoes, pail, bunting, shield, hatband
- ❍ 1/8 yard flesh for boy
- ❍ 1/8 yard gold for flag pole, straw hat
- ❍ 1/16 yard brown for hair
- ❍ Backing material 43" x 48"*
  *Measurement reflects 8" added to each side (for use in a hoop)
- ❍ 122" binding tape or 1" – 3" wide fabric to bind

To Make This Rug

- ❍ Enlarge this pattern 350%.
- ❍ Order: I started by hooking the boy, flag and sand pail. I then did the sky and sand - and waited until the end to do the patriotic bunting border.

Boy on Beach

ENLARGE 350%

OPEN

I PLEDGE ALLEGIANCE

TO THE FLAG OF THE

UNITED STATES OF AMERICA

AND TO THE REPUBLIC FOR WHICH IT STANDS

ONE NATION UNDER GOD INDIVISIBLE

WITH LIBERTY AND JUSTICE FOR ALL

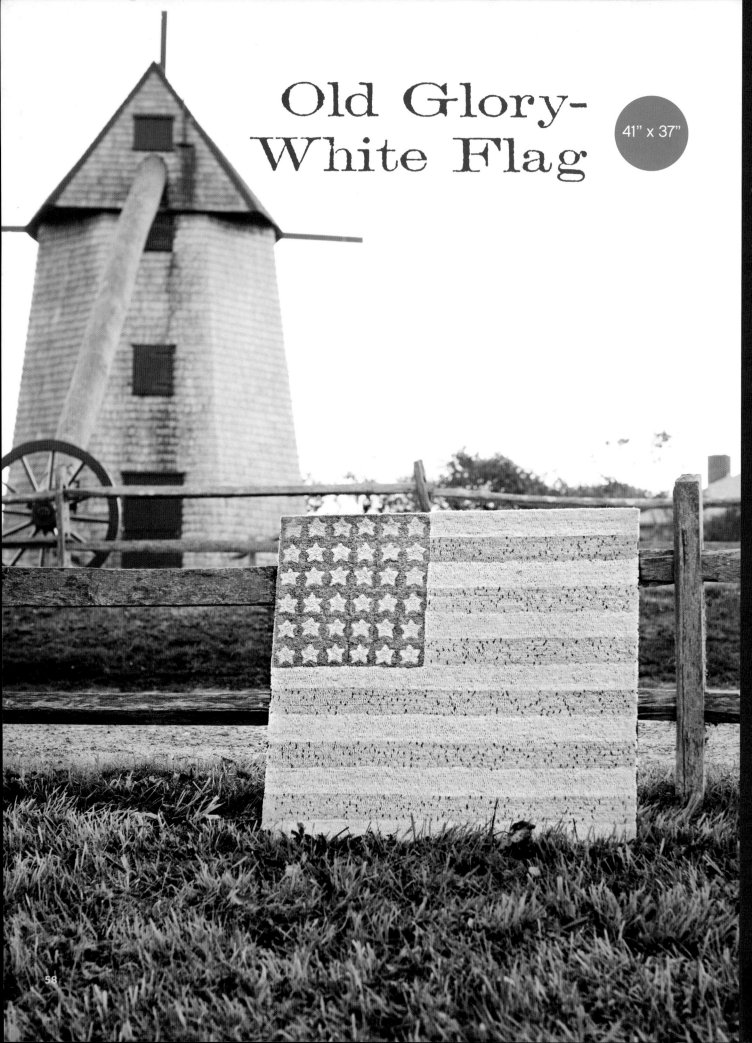

Old Glory- White Flag

41" x 37"

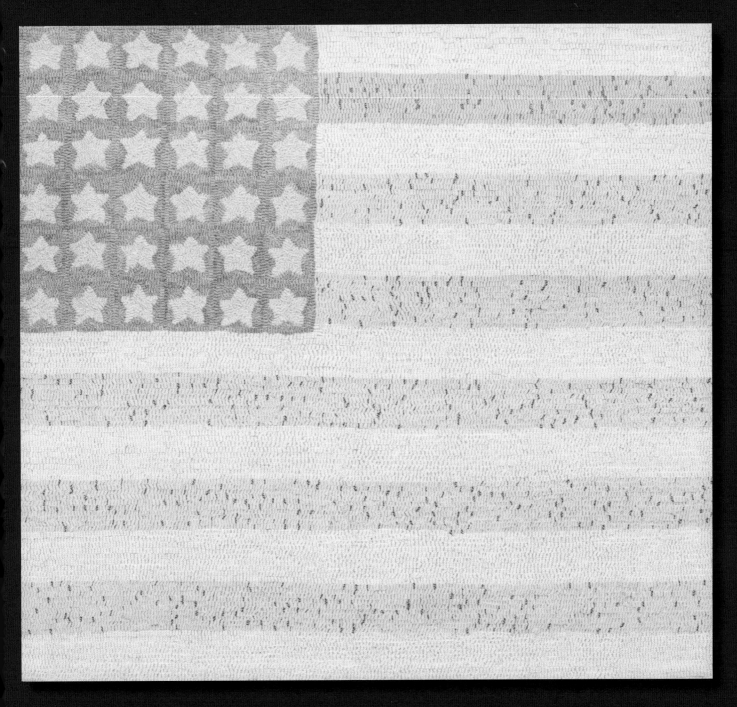

Flags have been a favorite theme in my hooking for a long time. I have hooked flags in many ways and in many color combinations. My goal is always to honor the flag. I have studied early flags made by sailors on ships and by ladies sewing. All have their own way to make our flag, all with honor. I decided to redesign my white flag in this larger size and style, and I am happy with the outcome.

Supply List

Note: all yardage refers to wool unless otherwise noted.

- ❍ 1 1/4 yards lighter off-white for bars
- ❍ 1 3/4 yards darker off-white for other bars and stars in canton
- ❍ 1 yard darkest off-white for canton behind stars
- ❍ Backing material 57" x 53"
  *Measurement reflects 8" added to each side (for use in a hoop)
- ❍ 160" binding tape or 1" – 3" wide fabric to bind

To Make This Rug

- ❍ Enlarge this pattern 530%.
- ❍ Order: I have hooked a white-on-white flag before, but this time I used the same flag design I usually use for another rug, Pledge Flag. I left out the wording and used all whites - all you need is a little color contrast. I do the bars in the flag first, then the stars and the background behind the stars.

Old Glory-White Flag

Mermaid 21" x 58"

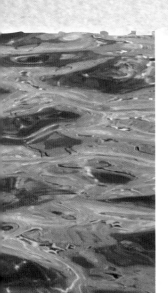

We have shown people on the shore, ships, lighthouses, whales - so why not a Mermaid? I hooked this rug for the Historical Society on Nantucket and when the photos of it appeared, I was bombarded with requests for the kit. Who knew that the Mermaid would be such a hit!

Supply List

Note: all yardage refers to wool unless otherwise noted.

○ 1 1/2 yards of soft blue mix for sky
○ 1/4 yard red for flag
○ 1/2 yard off-white for flag bars and stars in flag
○ 1/4 yard navy blue for canton in flag
○ 1/2 yard gold mix for hair, flag pole and
　star on pole
○ 1/8 yard flesh for mermaid
○ 1/4 yard turquoise tweed for halter top
　on mermaid
○ 1/2 yard turquoise mix - solids and textures
　for mermaid
○ Backing material 37" x 74"*
　*Measurement reflects 8" added to each side
　 (for use in a hoop)
○ 162" binding tape or 1" – 3" wide fabric to bind

To Make This Rug

○ Enlarge this pattern 600%.
○ Order: I started with the mermaid, then the flag,
　followed by the background of soft blues (so you
　can imagine it as sky or ocean).

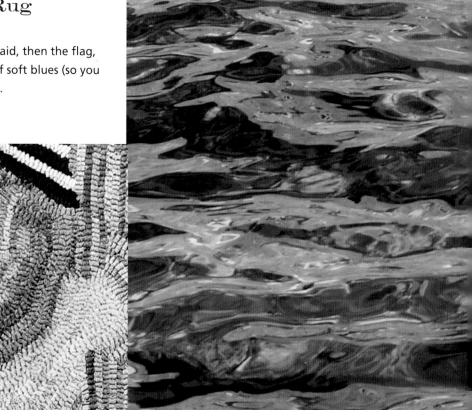

Mermaid 21" x 58"

ENLARGE
600%

Sampler Rug

29' x 35"

Since the rugs in this book scream summer, seashore, and the restful days of our American Summers, I really wanted to include this rug. The colors are summery and I have long wanted to design and hook a simple Sampler Rug. For that reason, I really wanted it to be in this collection. Stitched samplers can be found in early beach homes. Here's my version of the sampler rug. It is a favorite with my customers and I hope you will enjoy it too. It was great fun to plan and create.

Supply List

Note: all yardage refers to wool unless otherwise noted.

❍ 1 1/2 yard off-white for background
❍ 1/2 yard medium blue for alphabet
❍ 1/4 yard gold for outlining alphabet
❍ 1/2 yard indigo for house and one number and border
❍ 1/2 yard gold mix for star, heart, trim on house
   and a number or two
❍ 1/8 yard blue/white check for canton on flag
❍ 1/4 yard red for flags, house roof, number and star
❍ 1/4 yard white with blue stripe for windows
❍ Backing material 45" x 51"*
   *Measurement reflects 8" added to each side
   (for use in a hoop)
❍ 132" binding tape or 1" – 3" wide fabric to bind

To Make This Rug

○ Enlarge this pattern 375%.

○ Order: I started with the alphabet on this rug. I did not plan to outline the alphabet with gold, but after the letters were done I decided to outline them for better contrast. I also added the numbers after I started the rug as I felt there was too much background without the numbers. I did the house next, then the flags, stars and hearts. The background was last.

ENLARGE
375%

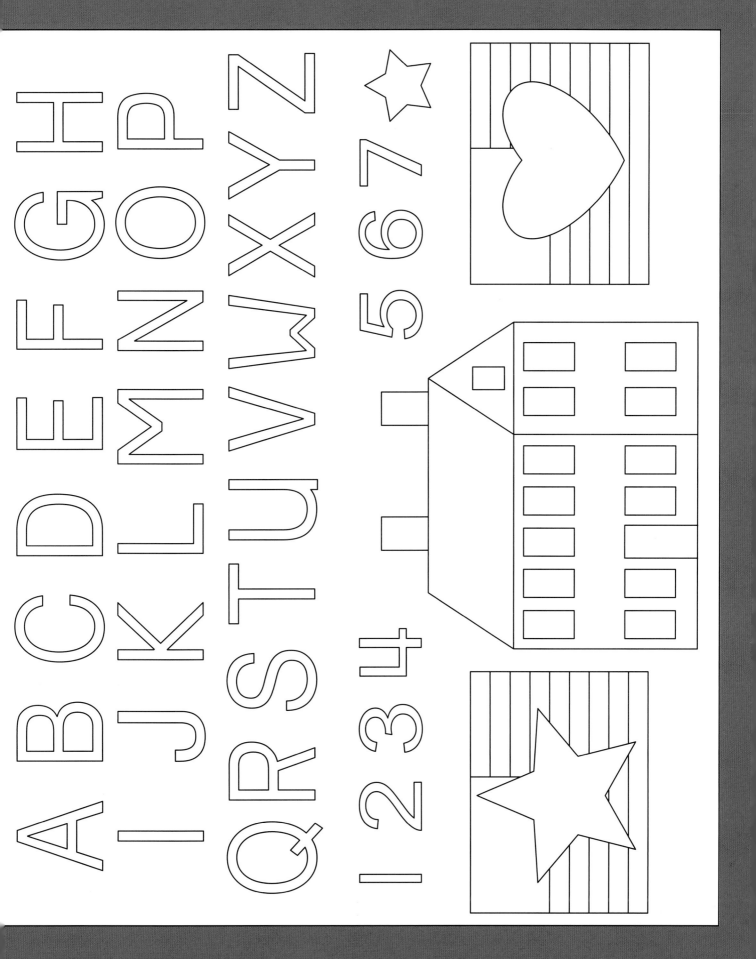

Big Fish

57" long x 22" high
(at highest point)

I had fun hooking this rug in a much smaller size for *Coastal Living* magazine a few years back. It was so popular that I wondered for a bit if I would ever hook anything else but the Patriotic Fish. One customer asked if I would hook it much larger - 6 feet long - and I agreed. I liked the larger size so well I made one for our home. It seemed fitting to include this in American Summer!

Supply List

Note: all yardage refers to wool unless otherwise noted.

❍ 3/4 yard red mix for stripes on fish, or soft blue - your choice
❍ 3/4 yard off-white for bars on fish and stars
❍ 3/4 yard navy blue for fish fins, tail and head
❍ Backing material 73" x 38"*
  *Measurement reflects 8" added to each side (for use in a hoop)
❍ 176" binding tape or 1" – 3" wide fabric to bind

Note: Because the fish doesn't have straight edges, it won't be easy to use binding tape. My rug is finished with ticking fabric to create a facing.

To Make This Rug

❍ Enlarge this pattern 570%.
❍ Order: I have hooked this fish in red/white/blue and blues and whites (see page 70) - your choice. I hook the bars on the fish first, then the head and tail. I decided I wanted to do this rug without background and enjoyed doing it - I wanted a uniquely shaped rug.

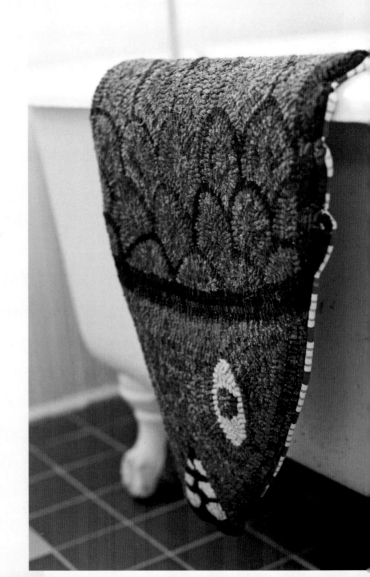

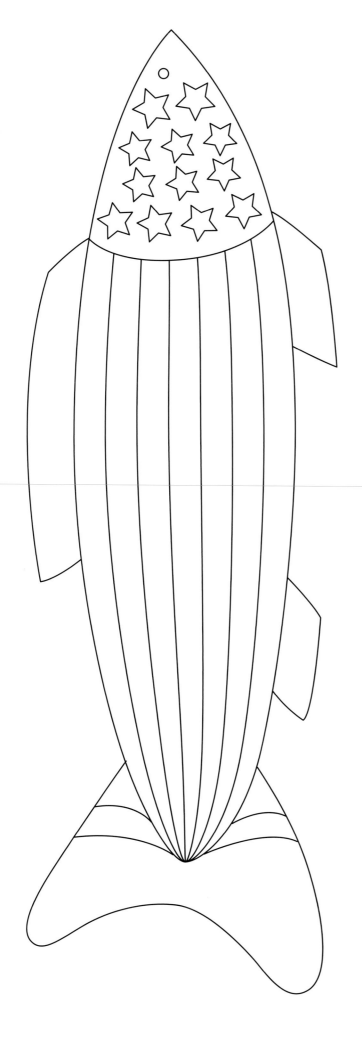

Big Fish

ENLARGE 570%

Quilts

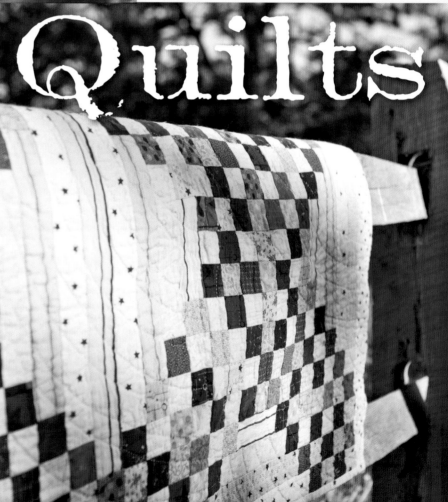

Patriotic Constellation

116 1/2" x 116 1/2"
Corner small star block - 10" square
Stitched by Laurie Simpson, machine quilted by Kari Smith-Ruedisale

My inspiration for this came when I spied an antique quilt - or a peek of half of one - in an older issue of *Quiltmania* magazine. I looked at the photo of one side of the quilt and got out my graph paper and tried to re-create it. This is the result. My original reproduction was made of mid-19th century fabrics. I thought a lighter, airier version would be fun.

Materials

Note - Fabric letter designations are listed for ease in cutting and piecing the large center star.

- ❍ 6 - 1/2 yard pieces of assorted prints for small stars, medium size stars, and fabrics A, B, C, U, V, and W for the large star
- ❍ 2 - 2/3 yard pieces of assorted prints for small stars, medium size stars, and fabrics D and T for the large star
- ❍ 2 - 3/4 yard pieces of assorted prints for small stars, medium size stars, and fabrics E and S for the large star
- ❍ 4 - 7/8 yard pieces of assorted prints for small stars, medium size stars, and fabrics F, G, Q, and R for the large star
- ❍ 4 - 1 yard pieces of assorted prints for small stars, medium size stars, and fabrics H, I, O, and P for the large star
- ❍ 2 - 1 1/8 yard pieces of assorted prints for small stars, medium size stars, and fabrics J and N for the large star
- ❍ 3 - 1 1/4 yard pieces of assorted prints for small stars, medium size stars, and fabrics K, L, and M for the large star
- ❍ 5 - 1/3 yard pieces of assorted prints for small stars, and medium size stars
- ❍ 2 3/4 yards light print for background
- ❍ 1 yard light fabric for binding
- ❍ 10 1/4 yards backing fabric
- ❍ 123" square batting
- ❍ Spray starch or Best Press Starch Alternative

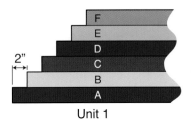

Unit 1

Unit 2

Unit 3

Unit 4

Unit 5

Unit 6

Diagram 1

Cutting

Cut pieces in the order that follows in each section. To help keep the fabrics stable, spray the fabrics with starch and press them before cutting. Also, starch and press after every step in the construction process. You want your fabric to act more like light cardboard than fabric to help keep all the bias edges from stretching. Once these strips are cut - label them by their letter.

Cut Fabric for the Large Center Star

❍ From each of fabrics A and W, cut: 1 - 2 1/2" x 42" strip
❍ From each of fabrics B and V, cut: 2 - 2 1/2" x 42" strips
❍ From each of fabrics C and U, cut: 3 - 2 1/2" x 42" strips
❍ From each of fabrics D and T, cut: 4 - 2 1/2" x 42" strips
❍ From each of fabrics E and S, cut: 5 - 2 1/2" x 42" strips
❍ From each of fabrics F and R, cut: 6 - 2 1/2" x 42" strips
❍ From each of fabrics G and Q, cut: 7 - 2 1/2" x 42" strips
❍ From each of fabrics H and P, cut: 8 - 2 1/2" x 42" strips
❍ From each of fabrics I and O, cut: 9 - 2 1/2" x 42" strips
❍ From each of fabrics J and N, cut: 10 - 2 1/2" x 42" strips
❍ From each of fabrics K and M, cut: 11 - 2 1/2" x 42" strips
❍ From fabric L, cut: 12 - 2 1/2" x 42" strips

Assembly

1. Assemble the Large Center Star. *Note: 4 large diamonds - 1 lower, 2 middle, and 1 upper (see diagram 6 on page 80) - compose each point of the large center star.*
2. Referring to Diagram 1, arrange 2 1/2" x 42" strips in 6 units as shown, offsetting strips by 2". Letters indicate which fabrics to use.
3. Sew together strips in each unit. Press seams away from bottom strip, pressing after each seam is sewn. Take care to sew accurate 1/4" seams to avoid a distorted or wavy star. Check width of strips in completed units. Inside strips should be exactly 2" from seam line to seam line, and outer strips should be 2 1/4" wide.
4. Rotate each unit 180 degrees, then trim the right-hand edge at a 45 degree angle (Diagram 2). To easily trim at this angle, first align the 45 degree line of a square acrylic ruler with a seam on the unit. Abut the edge of a 6" x 24" acrylic ruler with the square ruler; trim.

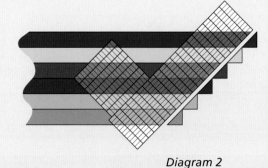

Diagram 2

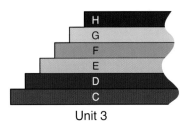
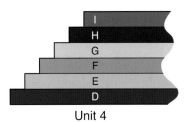
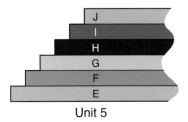
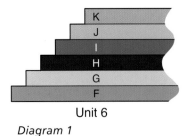

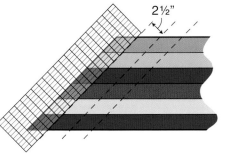

Diagram 3

2½"

5. Again rotate each unit 180 degrees. Cutting parallel to the trimmed left-hand edge, cut each unit into 8 - 2 1/2" wide sections to make diamond rows (Diagram 3). Check every 2 or 3 rows to ensure you're still cutting at a perfect 45 degree angle. Repeat Step 3 to correct the angle, if needed. Keep diamond rows stacked and labeled by unit.

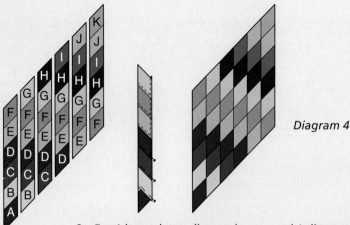

Diagram 4

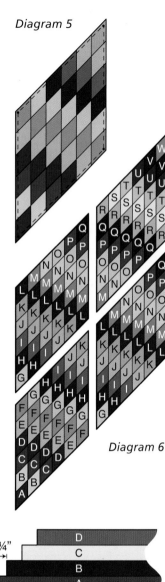

Diagram 5

Diagram 6

6. For 1 lower large diamond, you need 1 diamond row from each unit. Lay out diamond rows (Diagram 4). Layer diamond rows from units 1 and 2 with right sides together. Pin rows together, inserting pins into 1/4" seams and being careful to intersect seam lines. A small amount of fabric will extend at top and bottom. Slowly sew together rows, removing each pin just before you reach it. Join diamond rows from units 3 and 4 and from unit 5 and 6 in the same manner. Joint paired rows to make a lower large diamond. Press seams in one direction; do not press the seams open.

7. On the lower large diamond, mark a dot in each corner where 1/4" seam allowances intersect (Diagram 5). The dots indicate where seams should stop and start when the diamond is joined to another. To set in the large center star corner blocks, do not sew into seam allowances beyond these dots.

8. Repeat steps 5 and 6 to make and mark 8 lower large diamonds total.

9. Referring to Diagram 6 for fabric placement, repeat steps 1 through 6 to make and mark 16 middle large diamonds total.

10. Referring to Diagram 6 for fabric placement, repeat steps 1 through 6 to make and mark 8 upper large diamonds total.

11. Join 1 lower large diamond, 2 middle large diamonds, and 1 upper large diamond to make a large diamond point (Diagram 6). Press seams open. Repeat to make 8 large diamond points total.

Cut and Assemble Medium Stars

The following instructions result in a set of 8 matching medium diamond points. Repeat cutting and assembly instructions to make 6 sets total (48 medium diamond points). From scraps of already cut fabrics and from remaining prints, choose 7 fabrics to make each set, designating them as fabrics A through G.

❍ From each of fabrics A and G, cut: 1 - 2 1/4" x 42" strip
❍ From each of fabrics B and F, cut: 2 - 2 1/4" x 42" strips
❍ From each of fabrics C and E, cut: 3 - 2 1/4" x 42" strips
❍ From fabric D, cut: 4 - 2 1/4" x 42" strips

1. Referring to Diagram 7, arrange 2 1/4" x 42" strips in 4 units as shown, offsetting strips by 1 3/4". Sew together strips in each unit. Press seams away from the bottom strip.

Diagram 7

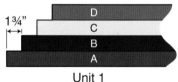

Unit 1

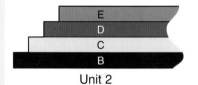

Unit 2

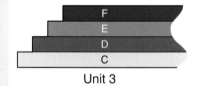

Unit 3

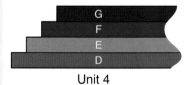

Unit 4

80

2. Referring to Assemble Large Star Diamond Points, steps 3 and 4, trim edge of each unit, then cut each unit into 8 - 2 1/4" wide diamond rows. Sew together diamond rows as before to make a small diamond point (Diagram 8). Press seams in one direction.

3. Referring to Assemble Large Star Diamond Points, Step 6, mark a dot in each corner of the small diamond point where 1/4" seam allowances intersect.

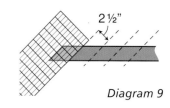

Diagram 8

4. Repeat steps 1, 2 and 3 to make and mark 32 small diamond points total.

5. Make 16 small diamond points for the 4 side half star units.

Cut and Assemble Small Star blocks and Setting Units

1. From scraps of already cut fabrics and remaining prints, cut 36 - 2 1/2" x 42" strips, cutting each strip into 8 - 2 1/2" diamonds (see Diagram 9; you will have 36 sets of 8 matching pieces).

Diagram 9

2. From the light print, cut 52 - 5 5/8" squares, cutting each in half diagonally twice for 208 triangles total. Also cut 112 - 3 1/2" squares.

3. Sew together 2 matching diamonds, without sewing into 1/4" seam allowance, to make an angled unit. Finger press seam open. Referring to Diagram 10, set a light print triangle into angled unit to make a star point unit: the light print triangle will extend slightly beyond edges of star point unit. Press seams toward light print triangle. Repeat to make 4 matching star point units total.

Diagram 10

4. Referring to Diagram 11 and without sewing into 1/4" seam allowance, join 2 star point units. Set a light print 3 1/2" square into corner between star point units to make a star half. Press seams toward light print square. Repeat to make a second star half.

Diagram 11

5. Sew together 2 star halves without sewing into 1/4" seam allowance. Press seam open. Set light print 3 1/2" squares into open corners (Diagram 12) to make a small star block. Press seams toward light print squares. The block should be 10 1/2" square including seam allowances. Note: The star should "float" slightly with the light prints.

6. Repeat steps 1 through 3 to make 20 small star blocks total.

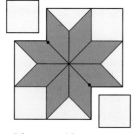

Diagram 12

7. Repeat steps 1 and 2 to make 2 matching star halves. Sew light print triangles to opposite edges of each star half to make small star setting units (Diagram 13). Press seams toward light print triangles. Repeat to make 32 small star setting units total.

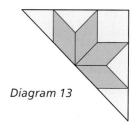

Diagram 13

Assemble Quilt Top

1. Stitching from dot to dot, sew together 2 matching medium diamond points to make an angled unit. Press seam open. Set a small star setting unit into angled unit to make a medium diamond pair; the setting unit will extend slightly beyond edges. Repeat to make 4 matching medium diamond pairs total.

2. Referring to Diagram 14, lay out 4 medium diamond pairs and 4 small star blocks. Join medium diamond pairs into star halves and set in small star blocks; press seams toward small star blocks.

Diagram 15

Diagram 14

3. Sew together star halves and set in the remaining 2 small star blocks to make a medium star corner block; press seams toward small star blocks. If necessary, trim the corner block to 34 1/2" square including seam allowances (Diagram 15). *Note: The medium star might "float" slightly within the corner block.*

4. Repeat steps 1 through 3 to make 4 medium corner blocks total.

5. Repeat steps 1 and 2 to make 2 matching star halves. Sew small star setting units to opposite edges of each half medium star to make a half medium star setting unit. (Diagram 16). Press seams toward the small star setting units. Repeat to make 4 half medium setting units total.

6. Stitching from dot to dot, sew together 2 large diamond points to make an angled unit (see Assembly Diagram). Press seam open. Set a half medium star setting unit into angled unit to make a large diamond pair; the setting unit will extend slightly beyond edges. Repeat to make 4 large diamond pairs total.

7. Stitching from dot to dot, join 2 large diamond pairs to make a half star. Repeat to make a second half star.

8. Stitching from dot to dot, sew together half stars to complete large star.

9. Set medium corner blocks into the large star to complete the quilt top.

Diagram 16

Assembly Diagram

85 1/2" x 85 1/2"
Stitched by Laurie Simpson,
quilted by Kari Smith-Ruedisale

This quilt was inspired by
a piece of Japanese fabric
that I found on sale. It is
a lovely, washed out floral
with splashes of red and pale pink against a wonderful Japanese neutral. I have long
been enamored of the subtlety and beauty achieved with these neutral fabrics and this
was a small attempt to merge that Japanese aesthetic and antique American quilts.

Summer Roses

Materials Needed

- ❍ 6 yards neutral fabric
- ❍ 3 1/2 yards neutral floral fabric
- ❍ 1 3/4 yards assorted blues for stems and leaves
- ❍ 1/2 yard assorted reds for flowers
- ❍ 2/3 yard red fabric for binding.

Cutting For Applique
Templates are on page 88.

- ❍ Large Flowers: Cut 16 from assorted blue fabric
- ❍ Medium Flowers: Cut 16 from assorted blue fabric and
  12 from assorted red fabric
- ❍ Small Flowers: Cut 16 from assorted blue fabric
- ❍ Flower Circle Centers: Cut 12 from assorted blue fabric
- ❍ Large Lobed Leaf: Cut 4 and 4(reversed)
  from assorted blue fabric
- ❍ Medium Leaf: Cut 13 from assorted blue fabric
- ❍ Small Leaf: Cut 3 from assorted blue fabric
- ❍ Top Stem: Cut 4 and 4(r) from the bias stem fabric
- ❍ Bud Leaf: Cut 4 and 4(r) from assorted blue fabric
- ❍ Bud: Cut 4 and 4(r) from assorted red fabric
- ❍ Flower Pot: Cut 4 from assorted red fabric
- ❍ 100" - 3/4" wide bias for 4 center stems and 24 short stems
- ❍ 3/8" bias tape maker

For Pieced Background

Neutral

- ○ 4 - 18 1/2" squares
- ○ 12 - 8" x 18 1/2" rectangles
- ○ 4 - 8" squares
- ○ 21 - 3 1/2" x width of fabric (WOF) strips

Neutral Floral

- ○ 4 – 18 1/2" squares for appliqué backgrounds
- ○ 8 – 8" x 18 1/2" rectangles (D1 on Assembly Diagram)
- ○ 4 – 8" squares for quilt corners
(D2 on Assembly Diagram)
- ○ 21 – 3 1/2" x width of fabric (WOF) strips
- ○ 4 - 2" x WOF strips
- ○ 2 - 3" x WOF strips

Applique Block Assembly

1. Make the bias stems. *Note: It does not have to be continuous bias.*

2. Following the photograph and the diagram, applique the pieces in the following order, using a neutral 18 1/2" square as background: flower buds, leaf buds, small top stems, bias stems, center stem, large flowers, medium flowers, small flowers, flower centers, leaves and flower pot.

3. Repeat for the 3 other blocks. Press and set aside.

Background Piecing Assembly

1. Cut the WOF strips in half so they are 21" long.

2. Sew a 2" floral, 3 1/2" neutral, 3" floral, 3 1/2" neutral, and a 2" floral together into a strip set. Press seams to one side. Repeat for a total of 20 B strip sets.

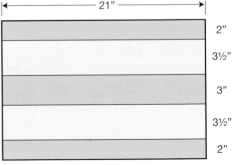

B

3. Cut these strip sets into the following widths: (12) 18 1/2" long; (12) 8" long; (18) 3 1/2" long. Set aside.

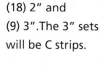
3½" widths

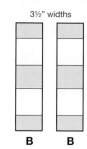

B   B

4. Sew a 2" neutral, 3 1/2" floral, 3" neutral, 3 1/2" floral, and a 2" neutral together into a strip set. Press the seams to one side. Repeat for 4 A strip sets.

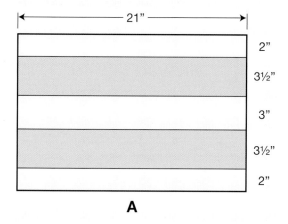

|←———— 21" ————→|

2"

3½"

3"

3½"

2"

A

5. Cut these strip sets into the following widths: (18) 2" and (9) 3". The 3" sets will be C strips.

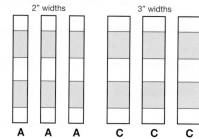
2" widths   3" widths

A   A   A   C   C   C

6. Sew these strips together (following the diagram) into an A-B-C-B-A unit. Press the seams to one side. Repeat to make 8 more checkerboard blocks. See Assembly Diagram on page 89.

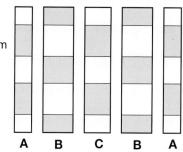

A   B   C   B   A

7. Once these checker-board blocks are made, sew the pieces into rows, per the diagram, making sure to orient the flower blocks in the correct way.

8. Once all the rows are sewn, sew together and press the seams to one side.

9. Layer your top, batting, and backing together and baste. Quilt as desired.

Appliqué Block Diagram

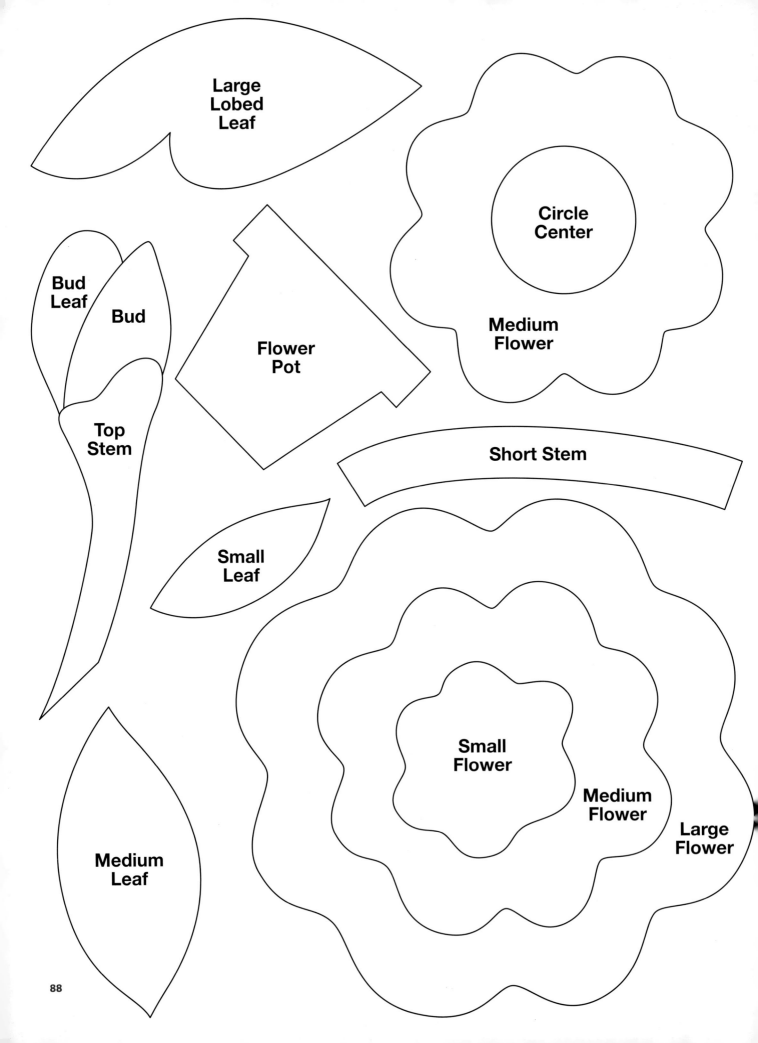

Large
Lobed
Leaf

Circle
Center

Medium
Flower

Bud
Leaf

Bud

Flower
Pot

Top
Stem

Short Stem

Small
Leaf

Small
Flower

Medium
Flower

Large
Flower

Medium
Leaf

Assembly Diagram

Checkerboard block

Summer Roses

Our Very Cool Bag

Many years ago, Polly's son and my nephew, Jim Minick, had a bag much like this one. It was a manufactured bag and it followed Jim and his family to the beach many times. Filled with canned and bottled drinks and a large bag of ice, this bag would keep beverages cold for two days. When it wore out, he challenged us to come up with another version of it.

This is what we came up with: a portable cooler that can be carried in one hand or over your shoulder. The water-repellant lining has NO SEAMS, so water cannot seep into the lining. We hope you like the bag as much as Jim does.

Supplies Needed

Note: our outer bag fabric and lining are both Moda's water-repellant coated fabric.

- Outer bag fabric – 1 1/4 yards
- Lining fabric – 1 1/4 yards
- Handle webbing – 120" of 1" wide polypropylene webbing
- Pocket – 1/3 yard
- 1 piece 40" x 43" insulation
  Note: We used Insul-Fleece Metal-ized Mylar Insulated Interfacing.
- 1 - 30" heavy duty separating zipper

Cutting Instructions

Outer fabric: Bag – 41" x 27 1/2"
Pocket – 9 1/2" x 7 1/2"
Lining fabric: Lining – 40" x 43"

- If fabric is directional, cut in half (20 1/2" x 27 1/2")'and turn one side in opposite direction – right sides together, and stitch 3/8" seam allowance. Finger press seam open and stitch the seam allowance down on each side. Remember: You can't iron coated fabric and if you have to rip out seams in coated fabric – the stitching holes remain.

Fold the insulation piece in half. At the fold, cut out 2 sections from each corner 5" wide x 4 1/2" high.

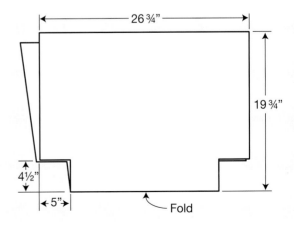

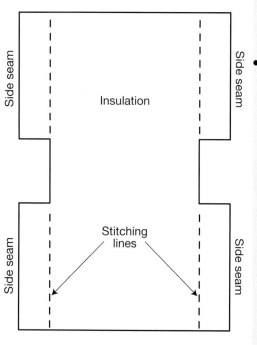

Insulation

Side seam

Side seam

Side seam

Side seam

Stitching lines

Fold outer bag in half and cut out the corners as shown. Put the insulation and outer bag together with the insulation on the wrong side of the outer fabric. Pin it together in the seam allowances (remember – if you pin in vinyl it will leave holes). Draw the stitching line from the corner cut out to the top of the outer bag. Stitch the insulation to the fabric on all 4 stitching lines.

On the pocket, fold under the top and bottom edges. Edge stitch the top hem only. Fingerpress the bottom edge.

←— Edge stitch

Pocket

On outer bag, measure up 6" from seam/bottom of bag and center the pocket. Pin it in place at the edges, as the edges will be covered by the handles. Edge stitch the hemmed bottom edge of the pocket in place.

Fold the outer fabric/insulation in half, outer fabric side to the inside, matching side seams. Sew along the side seam.

Side seam

Side seam

Side seam

Side seam

6" up from bottom of bag

←— Bottom of bag

Fold

Outer Bag

Now take the handle webbing - turn under 3/8" on one short edge and mark the halfway point (60") with chalk. On the outer bag, measure in 9" from each outside edge and draw a line with a chalk pencil. Starting at the bottom fold/seam line, place the unsewn edge of the handle on the fold/seam line and align the handle on the drawn line. The 60" mark of the handle should align directly opposite the starting point. When the other short end of the handle meets the starting point, cover the raw edge with the hemmed edge. Pin the handle in place all along this line in the center of the handle.

Stitch 5" from top

Stitched through handle, pocket and bag

Only hemmed through pocket thickness

Stitch 5" from edge

Start and stop tape

9" from edge

9

Measure down 5" from the top edge and bottom edge of the bag, and mark across the handle. Edge stitch the handles in place (go around twice to add stability). Sew in one continuous circle for each side of the handles.

To make the bottom of the bag, match the bottom fold/seam with the side seams and sew across, with a 3/8" seam, on the wrong side of the bag.

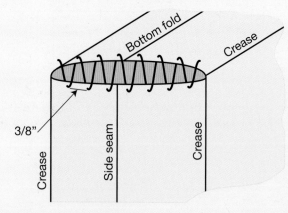

Bottom fold

Crease

Crease

Side seam

Crease

3/8"

Turn it right side out and fingerpress the corners down. Set aside.

Lining

Remember – there are no seams in the lining in an effort to make your bag water-repellant. This lining is made to fit inside your bag by the use of folding!

Mark the exact middle of all 4 sides of the lining with a small dot. On the outer bag, mark the middle of all sides with a small dot on the wrong side close to the top edge. Here's where it gets cumbersome! Put the lining inside of the bag with the wrong sides together – the long side of the lining matches the top edges of the bag. Match up the end and side dots of the lining to each other (pin in the seam allowance at the top edge). Now the folding begins!

Start at the middle of one side (matching dots) and pin the lining to the outer bag in the seam allowance. When you get to the corner, stop and begin re-pinning from the seam of the outer bag back into the same corner. You will have a large triangle of excess fabric. Finger crease it and smooth it back toward the bag center. Trim away the excess lining at the top edge only. Repeat for the other 3 corners.

The lining is floating and is not caught in any seams at this point. All excess folded lining is toward the insulation.

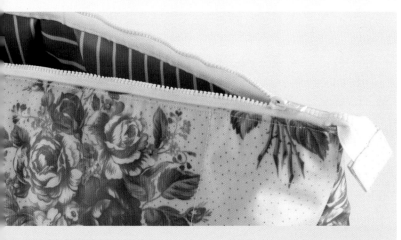

Zipper

Unzip the zipper. The bottom end of zipper should extend 2" beyond the side of the bag. The top end of the zipper should extend 2 1/2" beyond the side of the bag. Pin the wrong side of the zipper to the outside of bag with right sides together. Stitch the zipper through all thicknesses (not insulation) using a zipper foot with a 3/8" seam allowance. Repeat with the other side. Make sure the ends of the zipper are even. Turn the zipper to the inside of the bag. While turning, turn in the side seam edges where zipper doesn't cover. Topstitch in place all around the top of the bag.

To keep zipper ends from coming apart, cut a 1 3/4" x 2 1/4" piece of coated fabric. Turn under 1/4" on the 2 long sides and stitch. Fold in half and place over the end of closed zipper. Fold under the edges and carefully stitch through all thicknesses. Repeat with the other end of the zipper.

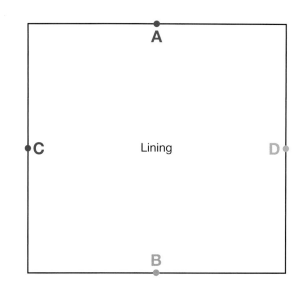

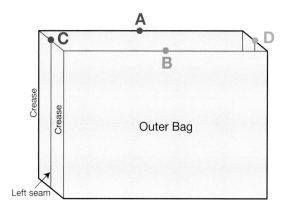

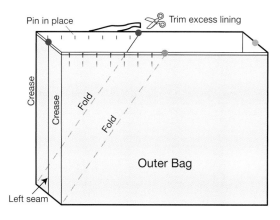

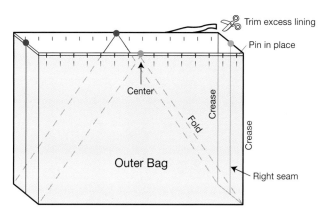

The Injured Marine Semper Fi Fund

The Injured Marine Semper Fi Fund was founded in 2003 as a non-profit group to offer immediate financial support for injured and critically ill members of the armed forces. This fund directs urgently needed resources to United States Marines and Sailors, as well as members of the Army, Air Force, and Coast Guard who serve in support of Marine forces.

This fund was formed around a kitchen table by four Marine spouses. So forever on, we can be grateful to Karen Guenther and her fellow Marine spouses – who responded to the need for this group.

When our son, Colonel James J. Minick, USMC was deployed to Fallujah, Iraq in 2005, I did what most Moms would do. I asked, "What could I send? What could I do? Could I organize sending boxes to his troops?" It is a natural and first instinct of a family member to want to help in any way possible.

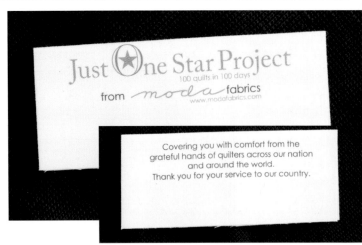

Just One Star is a program started by Moda Fabrics to make 100 quilts in 100 days for troops in hospital beds. The project went viral, and as a result, there will be closer to 1,000 quilts completed.

Jim quickly explained that his troops are well cared for and that actually they usually get more care packages than they can use and they often share with their allies.

He asked that our efforts go to the Injured Marine Semper Fi Fund, and he took the time to explain what this group does and the wonderful impact they have had on our troops and their families. So that is what we have done. I started selling my rug hooking kits with all money going to Semper Fi (all checks are made out to the fund). After Minick and Simpson was formed in 2001, Laurie willingly jumped in to join the effort to help her nephew and all those serving. We have worked extensively and with great heart for this group.

94

Representatives from Moda Fabrics teamed up with us to assemble rug kits to benefit the Semper Fi fund. Their donated materials produced more than 400 kits. All proceeds from those, several other kit sales and silent auction donations have gone to Semper Fi. We continue to accept donations for this cause so close to our hearts and thank the many, many people who have helped, especially the community of rug hookers who have generously purchased kits - many purchasing each and every one as they loved being able to help our troops.

Our good fortune was our partnership with Moda Fabrics! Not only to be included among their designers, but to learn of their generosity and heart. From day one, Moda has supported our efforts. With their help, we have been most gratified in our efforts to raise funds for the Injured Marine Semper Fi Fund. As of fall 2011, the fund has issued more than 34,000 grants totaling more than $54 million to thousands of our heroes and their families.

Thank you one and all -
and a special THANK YOU to Moda.

Learn more about the fund at
semperfifund.org.

My introduction to the Semper Fi Injured Marine Fund was in 2004. I was visiting wounded Marines at the National Naval Medical Center in Bethesda, Md. to thank them for their service and speak with their families. In an attempt to make their recovery slightly more manageable, I'd hand out magazines or snack food. No matter what we provided the Marines, my thoughts were of how insignificant and inconsequential our visits were. During one visit I talked with a sergeant in the Marine Liaison Office at Bethesda. I asked him the best way to provide support for the Marines and their families. Without hesitation, he said, "Donate to the Semper Fi Fund." He went on to describe how much they do for the families and Marines - that, in his opinion, no other organization comes close.

I've spent my entire career learning from Marine NCO's, so I filed away his comments as fact.

In 2005, during our first deployment to Iraq, my Mom asked what she could do to help. I thought back to my lesson from the Marine Liaison at Bethesda and replied, "Give support to the Injured Marine Semper Fi Fund." Our Marines in theater were getting truckloads of supplies and support. The ones I worried about the most were the wounded Marines sent home. Many were missing limbs or sight. Others had severe burns and significant head trauma.

What Mom and my Aunt Laurie did from there was beyond my imagination. They have built a bond with Semper Fi and continue to develop new and innovative ways to raise money and contribute to this noble and selfless cause. In addition, they have created an awareness for Americans who wanted to help, but did not know how. I'm always proud of my parents, and their relationship with this charity is another shining example of their gracious support.

Lastly, what I find most impressive is that my Mom and Laurie have worked diligently with Semper Fi for the last six years, whether my Marines were deployed or not. It confirms that when great people commit to a good cause, amazing things can happen.

– Col. James J. Minick, USMC